JUDI DENCH

Scenes from my life

Edited and Introduced by

JOHN MILLER

WEIDENFELD & NICOLSON

Preface by Judi Dench

Introduction by John Miller

1 MY FAMILY
and other animals 10

2 THE FIFTIES
Early steps: From the Virgin Mary
to the Old Vic 42

3 THE SIXTIES
The Company Spirit: First season with
the RSC; Nottingham and Oxford 54

4 THE SEVENTIES
The RSC and marriage, from
Hermione to Portia 78

5 THE GOLDEN ENSEMBLE
The RSC 1975–80, from Sweetie
Simpkins to Imogen 82

Contents

6 THE EARLY EIGHTIES
A merry-go-round: The RSC to
the National and the West End 98

7 THE LATE EIGHTIES
Carrie Pooter to Cleopatra
and *The Cherry Orchard* again 110

8 THE EARLY NINETIES
Mrs Rafi to the Countess of
Rossillion 124

9 SCREEN-SCENES
'Miss Dench, you have every
single thing wrong with your face' 144

10 MORE SCREEN-SCENES
From *Shakespeare in Love* to
Mrs Henderson Presents 176

11 SOME OFF-DUTY MOMENTS
'There aren't enough hours in
the day for me' 198

Picture credits 223

Preface

When I was first approached by Ion Trewin about putting together this pictorial history of my life, with the help of my biographer, John Miller, I don't think I quite realised how complicated such a task would be. I began by ransacking my cupboards and searching through the loft, finding some pictures I had totally forgotten about and failing to find some others I thought I had. I fear that some of the latter went up in flames when I had a house-fire some years ago.

Fortunately, we have been able to fill many of the gaps with the help of the archivists at the Royal Shakespeare Company and the Shakespeare Birthplace Trust, the National Theatre, the many photographers who have taken my photograph over the years and those friends who have snapped away more informally.

I hope the scenes that follow convey the pleasure I have enjoyed working with some of the most talented people in the business, and that they also capture some of the laughs we have had when we weren't working.

My eldest brother, Peter, is always trying to persuade me of the joys of retirement, but that plays no part in any of my future plans. Looking again at these pictures brings back many happy memories; yet they also remind me of quite a number of gaps in my experience which I would like to fill.

All my life I have tried hard to avoid being typecast or pigeonholed, and whenever anyone says, 'Oh, you shouldn't play that part,' it only makes me much more determined to try. Even dear Peggy Ashcroft urged me not to take on Lady Bracknell; other friends were nervous about me doing musicals, or against moving into television sitcoms. At the same time, whenever I have had a particular success in one role, especially in films, I am immediately offered several more exactly like the last one. After *Mrs Brown* and *Shakespeare in Love* I turned down several other queens in rapid succession!

I want to do something different next, and preferably something dangerous. Of course I have enjoyed playing some parts more than others, and which are which will become rapidly apparent in the pages that follow. Some made me laugh more than others too, and surprisingly often these were in the tragedies. I can't work unless I can laugh in rehearsal, as you will soon see.

I am glad to have had this opportunity of revisiting old stamping-grounds, and of recalling so many old friends. I hope you might enjoy coming with me on that journey.

Judi Dench

Introduction

When I wrote the biography of Judi Dench she was enormously generous both with her time and with her advice on which of her friends and colleagues I should talk to. So I was grateful for this chance to return the favour when she asked me to help her put together this personal pictorial history. As she says in her Preface, she lost her copies of many precious pictures in the fire in the house, but between us we have managed to track down many of the missing ones.

I already knew where some of them could be found in various archives, but her friends have also produced quite a number, which neither Judi nor I knew existed, and they show her in many different moods and costumes over the years.

The variety of her various roles covers an extraordinary spectrum. In Shakespeare she has given us a touchingly vulnerable Ophelia, a lilting Princess of France in *Henry V*, a mischievous Maria in *Twelfth Night*, a heart-stoppingly passionate Juliet, an imperious Titania and an Isabella in *Measure for Measure* who left no scintilla of doubt that she would rather lose her brother than her honour. Twice she has enchanted as Viola, and twice she has cast a terrifying spell as Lady Macbeth. A much rarer double has been both mother and daughter in *The Winter's Tale*.

She has impressed in roles she found unappealing, such as Portia and Regan; and triumphed in the most difficult and challenging, like Beatrice, Imogen and, above all, Cleopatra. Whenever doubts have been expressed about her capacity to portray such characters her determination to prove her critics wrong has always vindicated her casting.

After a long gap she reminded us again in 2004 of her mastery of our greatest playwright in Greg Doran's magical production of *All's Well That Ends Well*. Actors cannot flourish alone, especially in Judi's case, because of her adamant refusal ever to contemplate a one-woman show, like her predecessor Ellen Terry; and from the beginning she has acquired a richly varied roster of leading men. At the Old Vic these ranged from the matinée idols John Neville and John Stride to less likely figures, such as Tommy Steele and Frankie Howerd.

Judi has shown a particular affinity for Chekhov, in *The Cherry Orchard* (thrice), *Three Sisters* and *The Seagull*; for Shaw, in *St Joan*, *Major Barbara* and *Too True To Be Good*; and for O'Casey in *Juno and the Paycock* and *The Plough and the Stars*. She rose to the challenges posed by that difficult seventeenth-century quartet – Congreve, Middleton, Webster and Wycherley – and by those authors less familiar to English-speaking audiences than they should be – Anouilh, Arbuzov, de Filippo, Molnar and Pirandello. Even her sole stage appearance in Ibsen was in a play not seen in London for half a century, *Pillars of the Community*.

Her gift for playing stylish comedy brought down the house in *Private Lives* at Nottingham, and in *The Importance of Being Earnest* at the National; but she has thrilled younger and less sophisticated audiences too. First Field-mouse, Brave Stoat and Mother Rabbit in *Toad of Toad Hall*, and as Adriana in a romping version of *The Comedy of Errors*.

In modern work she touched our hearts as Deborah in Harold Pinter's *A Kind of Alaska*, awakening from years in a coma; as Barbara Jackson in Hugh Whitemore's *Pack of Lies*, destroyed by discovering that her friend and neighbour is a Russian spy; and as the fading actress Esme in David Hare's *Amy's View*, bravely carrying on working as her world crumbles about her.

She has revelled in parts which are nothing like herself - the coarse and drunken Christine Foskett in Rodney Ackland's *Absolute Hell*, or the monstrous Mrs Rafi in *The Sea*.

She always claims she is not a singer, but has had a whale of a time playing in several musicals - *Cabaret*, *The Good Companions* and *A Little Night Music*. If all goes well we shall see her in another in 2006 - a musical version of *The Merry Wives of Windsor* at Stratford-upon-Avon.

On television she made a huge impact as the brittle daughter, Terry, in the John Hopkins quartet *Talking to a Stranger*, and as the deliriously funny Lady Alconleigh in the adaptation of Nancy Mitford's *Love in a Cold Climate*. Some eyebrows were raised at first when she branched out into situation comedy, but the huge popular success of *A Fine Romance* and then *As Time Goes By* swiftly silenced those doubts. Judi rates sitcoms amongst the most demanding challenges she has faced.

It is hard to see how her phenomenally busy workload could have accommodated a career in films as well, but for many years that omission was caused by a mutual distrust between Judi and the movie-makers. That it was ill-founded on both sides was proved when she took the cinemas by storm as Queen Victoria in *Mrs Brown*, which won her first Oscar Nomination. She was nominated four times in five years. Ironically, she won the Academy Award for the shortest time on-screen in them all - as Elizabeth I in *Shakespeare in Love*.

We should not overlook her regular appearance as 'M' in the James Bond movies, in which her role became progressively bigger with each successive film in the series.

In Judi's own account of her life and career which follows, she characteristically makes light of her success, but it would be a great mistake to think that she is more concerned with the jokes than the quality of the work. The one makes the other possible, and I know from watching her at work on-set and stage how essential it is to her that she can laugh in rehearsal. It is that release of humour which enables her to give such searingly intense performances as Lady Macbeth, Queen Victoria or Iris Murdoch, to name but three.

The pictures she has chosen for this book capture her many moods, at home and work, and encapsulate what it is about her character that has gained her such a multitude of fans, of all ages and all walks of life, and now in so many countries of the world. I am happy to have played this small part in helping her to recreate these scenes from her life, beginning with what has always been most important to her — her family.

John Miller

1

My Family
and other animals

The love of acting is in the family blood. My father was a keen amateur actor, both my brothers acted at school and I followed my brother Jeffery into drama school. I suppose it was only natural that my daughter Finty should want to follow her parents into the profession. Though she initially wanted to be an acrobatic nurse!

At the Old Vic, 1957

My first ambition…

Becoming a dancer was what I thought I was really serious about as a child, I was always dancing everywhere. I can remember very clearly my father saying when I can't have been very old, 'The thing about being a dancer is that before you get to forty probably you won't be able to go on dancing, you'll have to do something like teaching it.' Even then, that was my idea of hell, and that really put me off. I don't like the thought of anything packing up. Until then I was really quite serious about wanting to be a ballet dancer. In this picture I am not conforming to anybody, I'm afraid, and if you look very closely you can see that I have extremely scabby knees where I was always falling down.

When I was a child, going to bed early in the summer was agony for me. I have such a vivid memory of hearing the boys playing cricket outside in the garden, then running up and down the stairs because somebody'd forgotten something and had to fetch it. Then friends would come over and you would hear a lot of laughing, then it would go quiet for a minute and you knew they had all gone off to somebody else's garden. I couldn't bear to miss it. I don't want to be part of the action necessarily, but I don't want to miss anything. I don't mind if I'm just sitting on the side, so long as I'm hearing it. I don't want to miss a lot of larks. On my right is my friend Ursula Gayler, who was later my dresser at the National Theatre.

The boy Michael Williams

This is the earliest picture I have of Michael (right) and you can already see his mischievous sense of humour.

'The thing about being a dancer is
  that before you get to forty probably
  you won't be able to go on dancing'

TECHNICAL DATA

Our wedding day – 5 February 1971

Michael flew out to Australia when we were touring with *Twelfth Night* for the RSC and proposed to me in Adelaide.

I said, 'No, it's far too romantic, with all this sun and the beaches. Ask me again one rainy night in Battersea.' So he did, and I said 'Yes' this time, and we got married in the middle of winter.

Tina Carr was a photography student when she took all these pictures of our wedding, when my brother Peter gave me away.

Two days after Finty was born

After Finty was born I was prepared to give up work altogether, but Michael preferred that I didn't. Fortunately I managed to get work in the theatre when she was tiny, so I was going to the theatre when she was going to bed, then later I did television during the day while she was at school, and had the evenings off, so I didn't miss out on anything.

'Fortunately I managed to get work in the theatre when she was tiny, so I was going to the theatre when she was going to bed'

In Cyprus where Finty learnt to swim

We were in Cyprus to shoot a magazine promotion for the TV series *Love in a Cold Climate*. There was a wonderful pool at the Dome in Kyrenia and the sea just washed into it. This natural sea pool, with crabs rushing across the bottom, was the most conducive place for learning to swim, warm and clear and sandy on the bottom. Finty learnt in just two days. She is as keen on swimming as I am and is wonderfully good at it.

Finty in her first communion dress

She was very, very cross about that dress, because all the other children were got up as brides in long white dresses and veils. I found this lovely Victorian dress and I made the bonnet, and Finty never quite forgave me for the costume. I thought she looked just terrific in it.

This was taken at Charlecote when Finty was three

It was so perfect. Michael's parents and my ma, Michael, Finty and me — all living together in one house.

'Wouldn't it be wonderful if we could all just live together? That was absolutely my idea of heaven'

Our extended family at Charlecote, near Stratford-Upon-Avon

My mother and Michael's parents all got on well together, so, a couple of years after Finty was born, Mike said, 'Wouldn't it be wonderful if we could all just live together?' That was absolutely my idea of heaven; it's like a Quaker community, both for bringing up a child and the whole idea of looking after your parents. It appals me more than anything else in this country how they are shot off somewhere where they sit like zombies in a room, and they're there to die.

This is a terrible picture of my ma. Michael's father is standing next to her. The very lifelike doll we gave Finty was called Daisy. Once, at an airport, Finty was walking along dragging Daisy by the arm and some Austrian woman came up saying, 'It's terrible what is happening to that baby, dragging it along the floor, it is shameful!'

We used to go on lots of camping holidays

We had many holidays camping in the west of Scotland. One year we got so soaked that all our changes of clothes were soaked too. Then I suddenly remembered that Tom Fleming had recently performed the opening ceremony of a hotel for Robin and Sheena Buchanan-Smith on the Isle of Eriska. He said, 'It's a wonderful place, you'll all love it.' So we went and threw ourselves on their

mercy and they said, 'Of course we'll dry everything off and you can stay.' The next day they said, 'Go off and have a lovely day; we've got another place for you to pitch your tent.' In fact we were put up in their house in Lymphoy and that's how that friendship began, and our love of Eriska. We've been going there ever since. We used to pile up the lilos and duvets in the back of the car, and Finty used to clamber in and just sleep on top of them all while we listened to the children's stories on the radio. She slept her way all round Scotland. We both have such vivid memories of being in our sleeping bags in our tent, and Michael sitting with a lamp and a vodka, reading us ghost stories. We had great times in the tent, until Finty suddenly developed a wish for a warmer beach. We were in a loch way up on the west coast of Scotland and it was paralysingly cold. Michael was shouting at us from the shore, 'You don't have to do this, you know, you are on holiday.'

Just returned from filming in Thailand

At Charlecote when I had just got back from filming *Saigon: Year of the Cat*. Finty came out for a while to stay with me and we had a lovely time; it was where she learnt to dive.

Returning to York with Finty

I was making a TV film about York, where
I was born. I took Finty to my school, and
the Shambles, and the Minster. The film
was called *Judi Dench looks at York* or some
such title. I have never actually seen it.

Michael with five of his school friends

Michael with four of the same group on his fiftieth
birthday. They all remained close friends throughout
their lives.

My birthday present to Michael

It's an armillary sphere, which tells the time like a sundial. I had it made for Michael with all our initials and names on it, and Sammy was born just beforehand, so his name was added. Michael loved it. Now, for my last birthday, Finty had a ring of stone put round it inscribed, 'When we are together, there is nothing we cannot achieve', which is something Michael used to say. When I came home for my birthday there were a lot of friends here and a trail of red wool all the way down through the meadow to the sphere; it was a beautiful surprise.

'When we are together, there is nothing we cannot achieve'

'Three generations
of Williamses when
Sammy was just two
weeks old'

Three generations

Three generations of
Williamses when Sammy was
just two weeks old, and eight
years later with Minnie, the
new Shih-Tzu.

The joys of grandmotherhood
Adjusting to having a new baby in the house!
Michael with Sammy on his first birthday.

We all loved Eriska

I took these pictures on the shore
at Eriska overlooking Lismore and
I love them. I think this visit started
Sammy's feelings for Scotland too – he
loves to go back there.

Michael and Finty
at Eriska

Sitting in the front garden,
having lunch, reading again.

Celebrating Sammy's
second birthday in New York

This was at my apartment in the Sutton,
when I was doing *Amy's View* on
Broadway. I adore this picture.

Dressing the part at Billy Connolly's

Sammy hated his kilt. 'Off skirt, off,' he kept saying, as soon as we put it on him. It was a bit better when he got the skean dhu. Now he's fine about it.

Sammy's first time as a pageboy

At the wedding of Sarah Kavanagh to Kit Bingham. He was told he could have Tracy Island if he walked up the aisle and behaved very, very well. The children behaved impeccably and all went absolutely swimmingly until he said loudly, 'Now can I have *Thunderbirds*, Tracy Island?'

Is this what you do?

My favourite picture of Sammy.
For a very long time whenever
you took a photo of him he
mimed what you were doing.

Our first holiday in Barbados

It was wonderfully relaxing. We read something
like twenty-seven books in this amazingly short
time. We just lay about, and read, and slept.

Relaxing at home

I have always loved living in the country.
We were thinking of moving from
Charlecote when our parents were no
longer with us, and Michael saw a picture
of this house in *Country Life*. He sent off for
the details without telling me, but as soon
as we walked inside we knew it was just
what we wanted. It's an old farm-house
with oak beams, which are a bit of a hazard
to my taller friends, and we have been so
happy here.

Even when I am playing nightly in the
theatre in London I like to come back here
every night.

Avoiding the sun

I wasn't allowed to get a
tan, because of a part
coming up.

We have always loved cats

Mitts, Spider, Newps, Fossil (in the barrow). Newps was short for
Newspaper, also known as the great flat-footed Newps. All the cats
have been great explorers, especially Fossil. As soon as I put him down
he was off into the wheelbarrow or whatever caught his interest.
Fossil was particularly intrigued by the egg basket. Fortunately he
never broke any of the eggs.

'All the cats have
been great explorers,
especially Fossil'

'Fossil was particularly intrigued by the egg basket.

Rescuing the ducklings

We woke up one morning and looked out to see all these ducklings in the pool. Michael had to go and fish them out, because they couldn't get out on their own.

Jonas

It isn't true that swans mate for life. When Jonas's lady flew off, he acquired a new mate in no time.

'Fortunately he never broke any of the eggs'

With Henry, our first Shih-Tzu

We bought him for Finty when she was little. We had to
call him Henry, because we saw him in a shop in Sloane
Street. He was adorable, and used to come and sit in at
rehearsals (sometimes!) with me. Now we have another
Shih-Tzu called Minnie.

'We had to call him Henry,
because we saw him in a shop
in Sloane Street'

2

The Fifties
Early steps: From the Virgin Mary to the Old Vic

The *York Mystery Plays* were revived in 1951 and were
performed every three years, directed by E. Martin
Browne. Daddy played Annas the High Priest. He
was a very good actor as well as a very good doctor
and my ma was in charge of making all the costumes,
designed by Norah Lambourne. We had auditions
at school, and I got in, playing an angel. There were
about eight of us from the Mount, and we were
allowed out of school to take part.

Ophelia with John Neville as Hamlet

The *York Mystery Plays*

That was a terribly exciting time. Tenniel Evans played the
Archangel Michael. He then went to Colchester and he wrote
to me all the time he was there; we had a wonderful long
correspondence until I was about eighteen.

Next time I played the angel sitting at the door of the tomb
in white clothing. Henzie Raeburn, E. Martin Browne's wife,
refused to let me have anything to sit on, so I had to crouch for a
long time. At this time I thought I wanted to be a designer, and
between my second and third appearance in the *Mystery Plays*
I went to art school.

Then I was taken to see Michael Redgrave's *King Lear* at
Stratford, so brilliantly designed by Robert Colquhoun, with a
huge saucer and a rock, which became, in turn, the throne, the
cave and everything else. I'd never seen anything like it and I felt I was very
old-fashioned about what I had previously thought. It was a Road to Damascus
moment for me. But still, when I come to do a play, the bit I like best is when they
show me the set and the costumes. Finally, I ended up playing the Virgin Mary in the
Mystery Plays in 1957.

Above As the Virgin
Mary, 1957. *Right* A
rehearsal break in 1951.
I am third angel from
the right, listening to
Tenniel Evans

With Jeremy Kemp on my twenty-first birthday

My parents gave me a party which was held at Queen Alexandra's House, by the Albert Hall, near where I was living when I was a student at the Central School of Speech and Drama, and Jeremy was also a student at the same time. On another night, when Jeremy and I were late back from seeing dear family friends John and Jean Moffat, the door was locked and we sat on the doorstep the entire night, until the door was opened in the morning. Jeremy stayed with me – gallant to the last.

'We sat on the doorstep the entire night, until the door was opened in the morning. Jeremy stayed with me – gallant to the last'

Ophelia in *Hamlet* with John Neville

I had this absolutely beautiful costume, designed by Audrey Cruddas, green shot with silver, and greyish silver beads. She set it in the Ruritanian period and all the chaps wore what we used to call shoes for tall girls – slip-on pumps. I got very bad notices for Ophelia. It did me a lot of good. If you get bad notices the first thing you do, it doesn't half bring you up with a jolt. When the Vic toured America it was decided that Barbara Jefford should play the part. That was hard to bear, but I was lucky enough to be playing Maria in *Twelfth Night* and the Princess of France in *Henry V*.

John Neville was playing Hamlet, and there is nobody who can hold a candle to John for leading a company – nobody I've ever met. He was brilliant at teaching you basic things that I don't think young actors are taught any more – the whole business of getting in on time, being prepared, and not taking up the director's time while you sort out the problem of what is actually your homework. He had a great sense of fun, which is terribly important, and there's no doubt that if a company is led like that it comes over to an audience that it is a unit which works together, and it's something you can't manufacture.

John used to hate it if anyone said they were tired and he's quite right. Acting requires discipline, and if they are too tired well, frankly, I feel they should let someone else do it. When I caught Asian flu during *Hamlet* at the Old Vic, one night I cried during the scene and went to pieces, and John came off and said, 'If you can't do it, let your understudy. Don't go on and show something that's nothing to do with Ophelia.'

I thought that was a very good lesson to learn.

'I got very bad notices for Ophelia. It did me a lot of good. If you get bad notices the first thing you do, it doesn't half bring you up with a jolt'

Phebe in *As You Like It*

I had a blonde ponytail as Phebe – what an arse-paralysing part! When the audience is shifting about and finding their handbags, ready to go home, suddenly she comes on again, having a row with Silvius. 'Oh good grief,' they all think, 'not another two having a row!'

Bottom left, with John Stride as Silvius

Cecily in *The Importance of Being Earnest*
with Alec McCowen as Algy

One night Fay Compton, as Lady Bracknell, said,
'Thirty-four is a very attractive name, Mr Cardew.'
Alec and I laughed so much we were told off by Fay;
we were really given a rocket. When I told John Gielgud
much later, he said, 'How dare she. She was absolutely
frightful at laughing on the stage.'

Romeo and Juliet for Franco Zeffirelli

The production was a great success. It was Franco's first Shakespearean production, John Stride and I were in our twenties though we looked much younger. We had a marvellous time doing it.

Left With John Stride
Below Franco Zeffirelli adjusts my costume

With Barbara Leigh-Hunt during the technical run

Her wig had obviously been taken away
to be dressed during one of the waits.

Maria in *Twelfth Night* with Joss Ackland
as Sir Toby Belch

One day in rehearsal Michael Benthall said to me, 'Could you
play it in a dialect?' and I said, 'Yes, I'll play it Yorkshire' and it
fitted actually very well. Joss played Sir Toby on the American
tour and he introduced me to jazz. Several of us went to hear
Kid Ory, Earl Hines, Louis Armstrong and Billie Holliday.

The Old Vic gang then and now

We recently had a get-together of some of us who were in the Old Vic Company at the end of the Fifties. In the picture of us then, I am on the left, then Maggie Smith, Moyra Fraser, Alec McCowen, Rosemary Ackland and John Moffatt. In the later picture Alec is behind me, Moyra sitting, then John and Maggie.

3

The Sixties
The Company Spirit:
First season with the RSC;
Nottingham and Oxford

The best work, in my experience, is always done
where there is a genuine company spirit. That was
something I learnt to treasure at the Old Vic, and
have since usually managed to achieve in my seasons
at Nottingham and Oxford, and subsequently with
the RSC and the National Theatre.

Isabella in *Measure for Measure* at the RSC

'One day I walked across the little bridge
over the Avon, absolutely howling, and
suddenly I met John Gielgud coming in
the opposite direction'

Anya in *The Cherry Orchard* with John Gielgud as Gaev

Michel Saint-Denis had seen *The Cherry Orchard* as a young boy at the Moscow Art Theatre. He had this memory about Anya and he wanted me to play it the same way. So I had a very, very hard time. I was in one whole afternoon saying, 'The birds are singing in the garden', because he wanted me to enter in hysteria, crying and laughing. I was in a terrible state.

Peggy Ashcroft said to me quite early on, 'Oh my God, Judi, I think you're going to be the whipping-boy of this production. I'll tell you something, never ever let him see you cry.' It was wonderful advice. Nor did I. One day I walked across the little bridge over the Avon, absolutely howling, and suddenly I met John Gielgud coming in the opposite direction, all muffled up. He said, 'Hello' and walked past me. We came to do a run-through and did Act I. And as we were about to go on for Act II Sir John said to me, 'If you'd been doing that for me, I'd have been absolutely delighted.' I'll never forget that minute and I think he did know eventually what it had meant to me.

Isabella in *Measure for Measure* with Tom Fleming as the Duke

When we were rehearsing at Stratford I used to cycle out to his cottage at Hampton Lucy for breakfast. I would collect the cream and Tom would have the porridge on, then we'd put the bike in the car and come in to rehearsal. On Shakespeare's birthday we were invited to that big civic lunch, and the beadle said, 'Name?' and Tom said, 'Tom Fleming.' The man announced 'Mr Albert Finney' and then he said to Tom, 'A horse, a horse, my kingdom for a horse.' We never did find out what that was all about.

Titania in *A Midsummer Night's Dream* with Ian Richardson as Oberon and Ian Holm as Puck

What thou seest, when thou dost wake,
Do it for thy true-love take.

I had one happy reconciliation during the run of *The Dream*. Franco Zeffirelli had been furious with me for refusing to join the Old Vic American tour of *Romeo and Juliet*, because I went to join the RSC instead. But now I had a letter from him, saying, 'Seeing how clever you've been in Stratford I have completely forgiven you for having abandoned Juliet. You know I've missed you deeply, I've hated you immensely — now I see that altogether you were right.' So that was good news.

Dorcas in *A Penny for a Song*
with Mark Eden and Michael Gwynn

At the same time as being at Stratford I was commuting to
the Aldwych. I was doing *The Dream* and *Measure for Measure* at
Stratford, and the TV of *Major Barbara* in London. We seemed
to be going up and down the road from London to Stratford
about three times every other day. We thought nothing of it,
and there was no M40 then.

Barbara in *The Astrakhan Coat*

This was a desperately tricky play, a thriller where I had
to play Job Stewart's twin sister. I just don't know how
we got through it.

Margery Pinchwife in
The Country Wife with Harold Innocent

Harold played my jealous and puritanical husband
trying to protect his new wife from the lecherous
attentions of the rake Horner, played by Michael Craig.

St Joan at Nottingham

When we were delayed in Act II at the Dress Rehearsal I was standing in the Green Room, and I looked out of the window and saw a woman with two children and a whole lot of bags pushing a pram. I turned and looked at all this knitted chain mail on everyone and I thought, 'Oh God, what are we doing?'

It is at the hour, when the great bell goes after 'God-will-save-France':
it is then that St Margaret and St Catherine and sometimes even the blessed
Michael will say things that I cannot tell beforehand.

Amanda in *Private Lives* with Edward Woodward as Elyot

Noël Coward came to see it, but thank goodness he wasn't there on the First Night. My bracelet flew off into the audience, the lid came off the coffee-pot and Teddy put it in his top pocket; he pushed me into the top of the trolley, I couldn't get out and he wouldn't help me. It was the most riotous First Night I've ever experienced.

'"How do I come into this nightclub?"
He just yelled at me, "The way any nun
comes into a nightclub after hours"'

Isabella in *Measure for
Measure* with Edward
Woodward as Lucio

John Neville directed the play and
gave it a very different setting from
the one at the RSC. It was in
modern dress and the moated
grange was now a nightclub. When
I asked John, 'How do I come into
this nightclub?' he just yelled at
me, 'The way any nun comes into
a nightclub after hours.'

Irina in *Three Sisters* with
James Cairncross as Solyony

One of the happiest times I had was at Oxford and
making a friend of Frank Hauser. I did several seasons
at the Playhouse for him, with great friends like James
Cairncross.

He was a brilliant director and I once said, 'If Frank
asked me to step in front of a bus, I'd do it.'

Silia in *The Rules of the Game*

Silia was a provincial femme fatale in 1920s Italy and Leonard Rossiter played my jealous husband. Wonderful clothes!

'This was the first time that Ian McKellen and I acted together, though happily it was not the last'

Lika in *The Promise* with Ian McKellen and Ian McShane

It was a wonderful play, by Alexei Arbuzov, but nearly three hours long and only three actors, with lots of costume changes, and I used to drop off to sleep when Frank Hauser was giving us notes. There was a big bed I used to curl up on and Frank would say, 'Is she awake? Because I have a few notes.'

'I went for singing lessons to Gwen Catley
and after she'd heard me she said, "Well, yes,
you're not a singer"'

Sally Bowles in *Cabaret*

Hal Prince saw me in *The Promise* and my agent Julian Belfrage rang to say that Hal Prince wanted to see me for his production of *Cabaret*. I said, 'You have to be joking.' So Julian took me out to lunch, I bought a feather boa, drank two glasses of wine, and when I arrived at the theatre I sang from the wings. I was so frightened. Amazingly I was cast as Sally Bowles! I went for singing lessons to Gwen Catley and after she'd heard me she said, 'Well, yes, you're not a singer.'

I said, 'Well, I know.'

'But I can teach you to sing in your way.'

It was Hal who said to me, 'Read the book *Goodbye to Berlin*, and read what it says about her.' Of course, the thing about Sally Bowles is that she isn't a singer, she's a middle-class girl from England who's gone out to Berlin. She can't sing. She could never be a success.

The musical director was going to New York while we were rehearsing and he said, 'Is there anything you want me to bring back?'

'Yes, the top note from the end of *Cabaret*.'

Hal overheard me and he said, 'If you can't get the top note, act that you can't get it.' That suddenly released me. The one thing that Sally Bowles craves to be is a star, but it's the one thing she's not, she's a failure. I loved doing it, I loved working with Hal. When I was starting rehearsals I was sitting in my agent's garden in Primrose Hill with that beautiful actor David Hutcheson and he asked, 'Have you had the band call yet?'

'No.'

'When you have it, the hair on the back of your neck will stand up.'

He was so right, and it's not only at the first band call, but for ever afterwards. During the overture, when you are standing at the back waiting to go on, it's just so exciting.

I loathe taking curtain calls. It embarrasses the hell out of me. I begged Hal Prince not to have one in *Cabaret*, because I thought it would be so wonderful to have that train going away and everyone going with it.

4

The Seventies
The RSC and marriage,
from Hermione to Portia

I have such happy memories of the Royal
Shakespeare Company, first for Peter Hall and then
for Trevor Nunn. It was during my time there that
I married Michael and gave birth to Finty, and made
lasting friendships.

Hermione in *The Winter's Tale*

The Winter's Tale with the RSC

Trevor Nunn asked me to play Hermione and I was very shocked. I said, 'Good God, Trevor, all those juveniles have gone by, and it's mothers' parts already?'

'Yes, I'm afraid it is.'

Then about three weeks later he said, 'Actually, how would you like to play her daughter Perdita as well?' That had last been done in Forbes Robertson's production with Mary Anderson. The extraordinary coincidence is that the day before Michael and I were married, the critic John Trewin sent us a wedding present and inside was a picture of Mary Anderson playing Hermione. He told us, 'What you might be interested to know is that while she was doubling Hermione and Perdita, the only person to do

that before you, she got married. Not only did she get married in London, but she got married in the same little church in Hampstead that you are getting married in tomorrow.' Michael told the story in his speech.

I love that kind of continuity, of something being passed down, I love being able to pass something on. What upsets me about now is that I think the majority of young actors don't really want to know our great theatre tradition. I just think how lucky to be given the chance of playing great parts that other actors before you have played. So hopefully one is carrying on a great tradition, and I'm very aware of that. I feel that so strongly because of working with Peggy Ashcroft, John Gielgud and Edith Evans. They were all in a line with earlier actors.

Hermione with Richard Pasco as Polixenes.   Hermione with Barrie Ingham as Leontes and Jeremy Richardson as Mamillius.   Perdita dancing with David Bailey as Florizel

Bianca in *Women Beware Women* with Brewster Mason as the Duke

We had a banquet scene halfway through, and the food was supplied by Pargeter's in Stratford. By now Bianca had been seduced by the Duke and revealed that she was a bad character, and, as I had nothing to say in this scene, sometimes, when Lizzie Spriggs was talking I would get up and lean right across, take her chicken leg off her plate and sit and eat it. I had the most incredible time, just tucking into everybody else's food.

'I would get up and lean right across, take her chicken leg off her plate and sit and eat it'

Viola in *Twelfth Night*

Roger Rees and I invented a game called 'Ferret in the foot', also known as 'Badger in the boot' or 'Rabbit in the ruff', which had to be indicated with the appropriate action by different members of the cast. I don't think anyone in the audience noticed, but it was very exciting, and it didn't half get you through that interminable last scene.

With Donald Sinden as Malvolio

Donald invented a wonderful piece of business
on his entrance in cross-garters: he walked
forward and looked at the sundial, then he
looked at the sun, then he checked his watch,
then he moved the sundial.

In my dressing-room during the run of *London Assurance*

I had a lovely friend in Nottingham called Brian Smedley, who's a judge, and he'd asked me to marry him. I'd said, 'May I let you know?' The next time I saw him I was about five months pregnant. He just put his head round the door and said, 'I take it the answer's no?'

Grace Harkaway in *London Assurance* with Donald Sinden as Sir Harcourt Courtly

When we were rehearsing *London Assurance* Ronald Eyre suddenly suggested to me that perhaps Grace Harkaway should be short-sighted, and I found a tiny little pair of gold-rimmed glasses, which completely unlocked the whole thing for me.

Barbara Undershaft in *Major Barbara*

It was eight years since I had played the part on television, and Brewster Mason repeated his TV role of my father, but the rest of the cast were new to the play, though, of course, they were all old friends from the company by now.

With Juliet Aykroyd and Janet Henfrey
With Richard Pasco as Adolphus Cusins

Rehearsing in my Going-Away hat

Michael seemed to think it suited him as much as me, and I love this picture of him in it.

Portia in *The Merchant of Venice* with Michael Williams as Bassanio

Portia has a speech to Bassanio in the Caskets Scene:

I speak too long, but 'tis to peise the time,
To eke it out, and to draw it out in length,
To stay you from election.

One night I said, 'To stay you from erection', absolutely boldly and out front. Well, the wind band left the stage. My brother Jeffery, Bernard Lloyd and Peter Geddes all left. And I laughed. Michael had a great long speech as Bassanio. I've never seen him use his hands so much and turn his back to the audience; it was terrible.

I had this idea of a wig with lots of curls, and John Neville came to see it. I hadn't seen him for years, and he knocked on the door and said, 'Hello Bubbles.'

That's all he said to me, and quite right too.

5

The Golden Ensemble
The RSC 1975–80, Sweetie
Simpkins to Imogen

It was an exceptional time at the RSC, and it
is only in retrospect that I have heard it described
as 'the Golden Ensemble'. They were certainly
golden years for all of us.

Millamant in *The Way of the World*

Too True To Be Good with Joe Melia

During rehearsals we all went to lunch at Joe's house in Primrose Hill, and his wife Flora had a terrible headache, so I said, 'We all ought to go out and find a rare thing on Primrose Hill, and bring it back.' Ian McKellen and Joe Melia brought back a park bench.

Sweetie Simpkins in *Too True To Be Good* with Anna Calder-Marshall

I have a suspicion that some of Shaw is more fun to be in than it is to watch, and this play was absolutely heavenly to do.

Beatrice in *Much Ado About Nothing* with Donald Sinden as Benedick

I adored playing with Donald in both *London Assurance* and *Much Ado*. He is such a funny man. I had an argument with Peggy Ashcroft about Beatrice, because I think there is tremendous melancholy in her, and she didn't see any melancholy at all. Because Donald and I weren't in our twenties or thirties, we made it a last-chance summer that they could possibly get together. There is something very leftover about Beatrice. As she says, 'He played me false once.' She actually alludes to that, so I took that as my guide, that she was hurt badly and didn't want to go there again.

I have to be able to laugh in rehearsal

I don't want to work with anybody who hasn't got a sense of humour, it's too boring, and that goes for directors too. It's too tedious, there are certain aspects you have to take seriously, but the moment you start taking yourself seriously, and you can't laugh at yourself or see the funny side of something, I think pack your bag.

Rehearsing *Much Ado About Nothing* with John Barton and Donald Sinden

'The moment you start taking yourself seriously, and you can't laugh at yourself or see the funny side of something, I think pack your bag'

Lady Macbeth with Ian McKellen as Macbeth

I've never believed that one should suspect Lady Macbeth from her first appearance in the play. I don't agree with Edith Evans that there must be a scene missing, I can't see what it would say that isn't already in the play. I said to Trevor Nunn one day, 'We must do it so that any schoolchildren who come to see it and don't know it will think that that they may not do the murder.' We all take so many things for granted.

We did it at The Other Place at Stratford, which was then just an old building with a corrugated iron roof that used to creak and groan. Trevor

got the stage management to put little pieces of paper in every single chink of light there was, and as an exercise he sent Ian McKellen up some stairs and said, 'Judi, wait at the bottom, and Ian come down the stairs, knowing there are people asleep all around you.' That completely unblocked something for us. Trevor decided to do it without an interval, and we sat round in a circle on old orange-boxes, a very minimalised set,

and all our costumes were very plain. On the First Night there was an unbelievable storm throughout the sleepwalking scene, which sent gusts of wind under the door so the candle flickered, so it was effects by God, really.

We had no understudies at The Other Place, so when Roger Rees broke his ankle he had to play Malcolm in a wheelchair. At the opening of the play Susie Dury, who played one of the Witches, used to dribble slightly and drag her foot, two of the court used to raise Duncan up and help this aged person forward, so, after Roger had come on in his wheelchair, Marie Kean, the First Witch, passed me and whispered, 'It's the Lourdes production!'

We were weeping with hysteria, I don't know how we got through it.

Regan in *King Lear* with Marilyn Taylerson as
Cordelia and Barbara Leigh-Hunt as Goneril
The middle girl is wondering how she can play the rest of this part!
I should never have done it. I blame Mike Gwilym and Nick Grace
for putting me off Regan. I had a long fur coat, very Zhivagoesque,
in which I thought I looked very chic, until they said, 'If you run in
that fur coat somebody will take a pot-shot at you.'

Adriana in *The Comedy of Errors* with Michael Williams as one of the Dromio twins

We were never so fit as during this production, because of the class exercises that the brilliant choreographer Gillian Lynne put us through every morning. The open air taverna in John Napier's set looked like something out of a travel brochure for Greece, and I have never had so many letters from schoolchildren.

With John Woodvine and Barbara Leigh-Hunt

We have our *Lear* faces on. That rehearsal room is now the Swan Theatre.

Cornwall *Seek out the traitor Gloster.*
Regan *Hang him instantly.*
Goneril *Pluck out his eyes.*

I found it very hard to take the physical cruelty in Regan.

Lona Hessel in *Pillars of the Community* with Ian McKellen as Karsten Bernick
The play had not been done in London for fifty years, and John Barton cut it severely.

Ian and I only had three scenes together, and I remember I had to whistle a lot!

THE SUNDAY TIMES, JANUARY 22 1978

THE ARTS

Judi Dench and Michael Pennington rehearse the roles of Millamant and Mirabell for Tuesday's opening of Congreve's "The Way of the World" at the Aldwych. The RSC's new production is directed by John Barton and designed by Maria Bjornsen. Beryl Reid joins the company to play Lady Wishfort, with John Woodvine as Fainall.

Vive le style

Millamant in *The Way of the World* with Michael Pennington

This was the first time I played opposite Michael. Here we are struggling in vain to work out the plot, and I don't think any of us understood it. But we had great fun with it. John Woodvine had to hand someone something to sign and one night, instead of handing him a quill pen, he handed him a whole bird.

'I don't think any of us understood it.
But we had great fun with it'

Imogen in *Cymbeline*

This is a difficult play, and this was
my most difficult moment, when
I woke up beside Bob Peck's headless
body. The dummy's knees weren't
made accurately, and kept bending
the wrong way.

Below With Ben Kingsley as Iachimo

'The dummy's knees weren't made accurately,
and kept bending the wrong way'

6

The Early Eighties
A merry-go-round: The RSC to the National and the West End

It was Peter Hall who persuaded me to go to the National Theatre. Until then at the RSC we had always regarded the National as our rivals, but after Peter succeeded Laurence Olivier we all started moving between the two great companies as a matter of course. Now I seemed to be offered some very formidable mothers.

Lady Bracknell in *The Importance of Being Earnest*

Juno in *Juno and the Paycock* with Norman Rodway as Captain Boyle

We all had wonderful reviews for this. The day after we opened Trevor and I had lunch at the Café au Jardin in Covent Garden and he said firmly, 'We can celebrate just today, then we've got to forget it and start getting it better.'

Left With Gerard Murphy as Johnny Boyle

In costume for *Cats*

When we were rehearsing *Juno and the Paycock* I was finding it very difficult at one point and I said to Trevor Nunn, 'Haven't you got some mangy old cat that I could play in this musical you're going to do?' I said it as a joke and then I was cast as Grizabella; I was also going to play Gumby Cat, but I never played either of them in the end, because I snapped my Achilles tendon.

'Haven't you got some mangy old cat that I could play in this musical you're going to do?'

Lady Bracknell in *The Importance of Being Earnest* with Nigel Havers as Algy

I had no idea how to play the part. Peter Hall gave me two weeks off during rehearsals and we took the car up to Scotland and stopped at Inveraray for lunch on the way up. I looked at the Castle and thought of Margaret, Duchess of Argyll, with that very pale face, dark hair and red mouth. It was a great clue. There's also a quality in Lady Bracknell that could be quite predatory. She is so awful about Lord Bracknell and was always dying to get round to Half Moon Street to put her hand on Algy's knee. I had a more coquettish hat made, with a whole bird in it.

With Martin Jarvis as Jack Worthing

One night I skipped the line 'A handbag?' and I saw the whites of Martin's eyes! But he exquisitely came to the rescue and I don't think many of the audience noticed the omission, even though it's crucial for the last scene and the play. I got one indignant letter from a lady who said I'd ruined Christmas for her.

With Peter Hall in rehearsal

JUDI Are you sure she can be played at this age?
PETER I don't want you to say that again.

Deborah in *A Kind of Alaska* with
Paul Rogers and Anna Massey
All I remember on that First Night was that
moment of getting out of bed and walking
towards Paul as the doctor, and I had a clear
flash of thinking that's why I snapped my
Achilles tendon, so I would know the whole
process of learning to walk again. That stood
me in incredibly good stead.

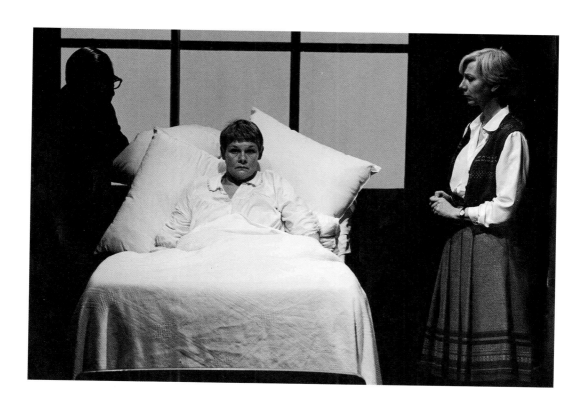

Barbara in *Pack of Lies* with Michael Williams as Bob
I adored playing this part, but it was very difficult. She was a very quiet and restrained person, so I found it difficult to pitch the performance to the back of the circle. Michael broke your heart.

'The wig should be red and look as if just anybody had cut it'

Mother Courage

I had clearly in my mind that the wig should be red and look as if just anybody had cut it, so it was always standing on end. When I said this to Lindy Hemming on the first day, she produced the design she had already done with red hair exactly like it. But the rehearsals didn't really work for me until I found Michael's old coat that he had worn in *Schweyk in the Second World War*.

Mother Courage with Bruce Alexander, Miles
Anderson, Zoë Wanamaker and Paul Greenwood
The wagon kept getting stuck, and only worked properly on about
ten out of thirty performances. One night I said, 'Look, we're the
RSC, not the RAC, so I'm afraid we can't fix this wheel and you'll
have to come back another night.' I thought it was quite funny, but
the audience were furious and they didn't laugh. Zoë was quite
wonderful.

'We're the RSC, not the RAC, so I'm afraid
we can't fix this wheel, and you'll have to
come back another night'

Amy O'Connell in *Waste* with
Daniel Massey as Henry Trebell
I lost my voice at the opening, until Cicely
Berry brought it back with some special
vocal exercises, to everyone's great relief,
especially mine.

7

The Late Eighties
Carrie Pooter to Cleopatra and *The Cherry Orchard* again

It is interesting, but often quite hard returning to plays from your youth in the maturer parts, moving from Ophelia to Gertrude, and Anya to Madame Ranevskaya. Both had such echoes for me, and I couldn't get Peggy Ashcroft's performance in *The Cherry Orchard* out of my mind. But Cleopatra was such a challenge – I said to Peter Hall, 'I do hope you know what you're doing, casting her as a menopausal dwarf.'

Cleopatra

Michael in *September Song* on television
I love this picture of him, and he had a huge success in that part.

Dr Watson to Clive Merrison's Sherlock Holmes on BBC Radio
This was a publicity shot for *Radio Times* and the only time they ever had to dress the part. It was a great partnership and the two of them were so brilliant together; the series ran for ages. They recorded a comic parody in which Sherlock Holmes confesses his secret love for Watson, which was never broadcast, but was played at Michael's memorial service.

Cleopatra with Anthony Hopkins in *Antony and Cleopatra*

I will never forget what Peter Hall said to me when I came to play Cleopatra, I have passed it on to so many people. He said, 'Don't ever think you have got to play all aspects of the character in every scene. Just choose one thing. At the end of the evening it might add up to the full person. The other thing is' (which would never have even occurred to me), 'don't imagine that when other characters speak about you, they are telling the truth.'

He gave the example of Enobarbus (which was so wonderfully played by Michael Bryant at the National) getting back to Rome, and that scene is really about him in the bar with his mates. 'Come on, tell us, what's she like?' He is telling a tale.

'Don't ever think you have
got to play all aspects of the
character in every scene.
Just choose one thing'

Carrie Pooter in *Mr & Mrs Nobody* with Michael Williams as Charles Pooter

Ned Sherrin was lovely to work with, precise, and funny, and very, very astute, then suddenly he'd sit back and say, 'Look out, the Williamses are on automatic pilot.'

We thought it was going to be a doddle, a really short evening, get a lot of laughs and straight home, but it was desperately hard work. However, working in those very heavy costumes meant I lost a lot of weight before I tackled Cleopatra.

Red-Nose Day for *Cleopatra*

No, I did not wear it on-stage!

Rehearsing *Entertaining Strangers*
with Tim Pigott-Smith

At the end of one rehearsal I told everybody
they all had to wear something red the next
day, and we'll see how long it is before Peter
Hall notices. He walked in that morning and
said, 'Oh, why have you all got something
red on?' All that effort!

'We have got to be serious, you've got to imagine that we are doing it for the Moscow Art Theatre'

Gertrude in *Hamlet* with John Castle as Claudius

That was the night I had a lot of people I knew in the audience, and I said to John Castle, 'We have got to be serious, you've got to imagine that we are doing it for the Moscow Art Theatre,' so we sat there solemnly and were all very well-behaved until Oliver Ford Davies, who was frightfully good as the First Player, came on, and John leant across to me and said, 'Has anyone told Oliver Ford Davies?'

John Castle on my left, then Guy Henry as Rosencrantz, Jeremy Northam as Laertes, and Dean Hollingsworth as a member of the Court.

With Daniel Day-Lewis as Hamlet

I thought, I'll try and play Gertrude like Jill Balcon,
Dan's mother, very tall and dark, but I never succeeded!

With Michael Gough as Firs in
The Cherry Orchard

Michael gave a radio interview just after we opened and said,
'I am working with three of the most attractive women in
the West End.' So when he arrived at the theatre that
evening I got together Miranda Foster, Lesley Manville,
Abigail McKern and Kate Duchene, and we all lined up in
front of him. I said, 'OK, Michael, who are the three?'
We never let him forget that.

The Cherry Orchard again. As Ranevskaya with
Miranda Foster as Anya

The play has such memories for me of Peggy Ashcroft when we were
at the Aldwych. Playing Anya first, then following Peggy as
Ranevskaya, and all those echoes of John Gielgud and everybody. It
was impossible to clear my mind of how Peggy had played it.

Finty in *The Mystery of
Edwin Drood*

Her first big costume part in a film,
and she had such a happy time with
Robert Powell. It's my favourite
picture of her in character.

8

The Early Nineties
Mrs Rafi to the Countess
of Rossillion

All my career I have wanted the challenge of doing something very different. I have loved to switch from the classics to new plays, from tragedy to comedy, and from straight plays to musicals.

Desiree Armfeldt in *A Little Night Music*

'Mrs Rafi was a deeply unpleasant character, and I got a letter from somebody saying how dare I call the play a comedy'

Mrs Rafi in *The Sea*

We couldn't get through the first reading, we
laughed so much. With twenty minutes of the play
to run after our final exits Celia Imrie and I used to
drink a small glass of champagne in the wings before
the curtain call. Mrs Rafi was a deeply unpleasant
character, and I got a letter from somebody saying
how dare I call the play a comedy. They had come
after a funeral and had expected to see something
rather different. Mrs Rafi was a monster, but it was
hugely good fun to play her.

With Karl Johnson and Christabel Dilks

With Michael Pennington
as Mr & Mrs Damson in
The Gift of the Gorgon
This was one of the most difficult
plays I ever had to tackle.

It had wonderful reviews, and Finty
was so bowled over by it that she
couldn't come round afterwards.
Because of the names of our
characters, and the fact that Michael
and I had played Mirabell and
Millamant, we always refer to
ourselves as Mr and Mrs Plum.

'This was one of
the most difficult
plays I ever had
to tackle'

Arkadina in *The Seagull* with Alan Cox as Konstantin

She is a self-absorbed character, and there was never an end to the things I learnt about her during the run. As I tackled Bill Nighy to the floor in one scene I would hear him whisper, 'Oh God!'

Absolute Hell

The play had been savaged by the critics at its premiere in 1952 and neglected since. The author Rodney Ackland came along to see the TV recording just before he died, and he said to me very touchingly afterwards, 'I didn't realise I had written such a good play.'

With Anthony Page in rehearsal for the TV production in 1991

I so enjoyed doing it that I said to Tony, 'Wouldn't it be lovely to do this in the theatre?' Four years later he and I did it at the National, with a different cast.

Royal National Theatre

Judi Dench by
The Douglas
Brothers

Absolute Hell
Rodney Ackland

Richard Addison	Alan Cox	Greg Hicks	Joanna Myers	*Director* Anthony Page
Sylvia Barter	Judi Dench	David Horovitch	William Osborne	*Settings* John Gunter
Elizabeth Bell	Kate Dyson	Corey Johnson	Mark Payton	*Costumes* Deirdre Clancy
Stephen Botcher	Alison Fiske	Edmund Kente	Anthony Renshaw	*Lighting* Mark Henderson
June Brown	Geraldine Fitzgerald	Richard McCabe	Penny Ryder	*Music* Jason Osborn
Sheila Burrell	Helen Fraser	Betty Marsden	Pip Torrens	
Judith Coke	Barbara Hicks	Marianne Morley	Peter Woodthorpe	

My favourite play – *Absolute Hell*

This picture says it all about the character. I would like to be going to do that play tonight. In the nightclub we were only drinking coloured water, but Greg Hicks and I used to get completely stotious, rolling about on the floor. It was like one endless party.

In rehearsal with Peter Woodthorpe

I loved Peter so much, ever since we were together at the RSC. He was wonderful as Toad. When he played the Doge in *The Merchant of Venice* he said to us, 'Well, I'm having strop, because Terry Hands has put me in this chair, and they can't see the cut of my costume!' He sat in it all through lunch, as a protest!

Backstage with Laurence Guittard as Fredrik

I fell down twice during the run. In 'You must meet my wife' there was one moment where Larry Guittard was crossing towards the band and I slipped, he turned round to face me and he couldn't find me. I was underneath the chaise-longue.

'I slipped, he turned round to face me and he couldn't find me. I was underneath the chaise-longue'

Desiree in *A Little Night Music*

You start to play a part and you get so immersed in it, trying to get it right, that you forget the responsibility of being passed that part to play, because it takes up all your energies and all your anxieties. We had a very merry time doing it.

Esme in *Amy's View*

I loved playing Esme in David Hare's play at the National and
then had a thrilling time on Broadway with it, but it didn't
start out like that. For the very first time in my career I found I
couldn't just pick up the lines in rehearsal and had to really
work at it. I used to come home, say hello to Mike, go up and
run a bath, and get into the bath with the script. I would spend
an hour in the bath, just trying to learn a page. I don't like
working like that, but it was a necessity.

Below With Samantha Bond as my daughter Amy.

'I would spend an hour in the bath,
just trying to learn a page'

Making up for *Amy's View*

John Timbers took this picture the night before I flew off to my first Oscar ceremony.

In rehearsal for *Amy's View* with Richard Eyre and David Hare

David attended nearly all the rehearsals and was a most encouraging audience for us, as he laughed at all the jokes.

Filumena with Michael Pennington as Domenico

I had a line, 'I don't suppose you know those hovels in San Giviniello, in Vergine, in Forcella, Tribunale, Palinetto…' and I totally dried on the First Night. Fortunately I had just come back from filming *Tea with Mussolini* in Italy, so I said instead, '…in Fuseli, Vermicelli, Valpolicella…' a lot of wine and food, mostly pasta, because I'd been having it for nearly three months. Not many people seemed to notice, but a couple of the critics recognised that something had gone wrong. The rest of the run was fine and we played to packed houses.

The Countess of Rossillion in *All's Well That Ends Well*

I hadn't been back to Stratford in a play for more than twenty years and it was Finty who talked me into it. She said she had such happy memories of growing up there that she wanted Sammy to have the same experience. We had one of the happiest Christmases at Stratford, certainly since Michael died, and we felt very near him at Charlecote.

Screen-scenes

'Miss Dench you have every single thing wrong with your face'

That was the crushing verdict of the film producer who gave me my very first screen test back in the 1950s. It put me off films for a long time, and my few early excursions into the cinema did little to change my mind. Television seemed to be much more fun, from an early *Z-Cars* episode to the later situation comedies I so enjoyed. Even my first big-screen success began life as a project for TV.

Queen Victoria in *Mrs Brown*

'That film was shot in Deodar Road in Putney, directly under the flight path, directly next to the road bridge, directly next to the railway bridge'

As Jude in *Four in the Morning*

That film was shot in Deodar Road in Putney, directly under the flight path, directly next to the road bridge, directly next to the railway bridge, and opposite where they dumped the rubbish on the river. We never got a take for longer than a minute and a half.

It was just after the shooting of this that my father died. Norman Rodway came round for a cup of tea, and it was while he was there that my brother Peter rang to say Daddy had died. It was 1st December 1964.

On location in Thailand

With my co-star Freddie Forrest outside the US Embassy, and below, with the director Stephen Frears. Freddie had worked with Marlon Brando, who taught him to improvise his own lines instead of speaking those in the script. This didn't go down very well either with David Hare or Stephen Frears.

In *Saigon: Year of the Cat*

The film was shot in Thailand. We had a scene where we were evacuated in a helicopter, and the day before we shot it a helicopter had crashed on that very airfield, so Stephen Frears hid the newspapers from me. I would, in fact, have taken comfort from that, because if it's going to happen one day, it's unlikely to happen the next, is it?

As the Professor's wife in *The Browning Version*

I did this with Ian Holm in 1985 for television. I love that picture because it doesn't look like me, it just looks like the character.

With Ian Holm in *Mr and Mrs Edgehill*

It was filmed for the BBC in Sri Lanka and I said I could go, but Finty's birthday came in the middle of it and I was reluctant to be away at this time. Alan Shallcross offered to fly me home, as long as I worked right up to the moment I got on the plane, and worked the moment I came back. We had a wonderful birthday party and I brought Finty back some sapphire earrings. When I got back I was on the set within minutes of arriving. They built a beautiful house for us on the shore, which, of course, was demolished later. It was the most wonderful setting.

Overleaf Dancing on the beach in the evening

'We had a wonderful
birthday party, and I
brought Finty back some
sapphire earrings'

My first situation comedy *A Fine Romance*

It was directed by the divine Jimmy Cellan-Jones, who wore sandals the whole time, even in the snow. We were rehearsing in the church by Waterloo Bridge, and it was our wedding anniversary in February. Michael went to the flower seller under Waterloo Bridge and said, 'Could I have some roses?' 'Roses!!? D'you know what time of the year it is, mate!?' When I was singing one day in that church, the verger came up and said, 'Don't do that.' I never forgot that. Stop singing in church!

Above With Michael, Susan Penhaligon and Richard Warwick
Overleaf With Jenny Funnell as Sandy, and Moira Brooker as my daughter Judith in *As Time Goes By*

'"Could I have some roses?"
"Roses!!? D'you know what time
of the year it is, mate!?"'

The second sitcom *As Time Goes By*

Situation comedy is the most difficult thing I've ever done. You don't get a preview, you get one chance to get it right. In *A Fine Romance* Michael had a sure touch about it, he used to know exactly; and Geoffrey – if you want to know about playing comedy on television, just look as far as Geoffrey Palmer. We kept thinking we were doing the last series, but then Bob Larbey would write another one and Syd Lotterby always had such a lovely crew to work with. Even after we finally called it a day in 2002, we were suddenly asked back to make two Specials for Christmas 2005.

The most hair-raising bit of all is when you have to go out in front of an audience and say hello to them; that's more taxing than doing the rest of the show.

'Situation comedy is the most difficult thing I've ever done. You don't get a preview, you get one chance to get it right'

As Time Goes By

Geoffrey Palmer is fishing mad. In fact, it's often quite difficult to get him to work as he's always chasing the mayfly! So I bought him this special catch. It takes a lot of people behind the cameras to put even just a couple of us on the screen. On the next page you can see how many. The director Syd Lotterby (in the armchair front left) managed to get most of the same team together for each series, and a lot of them came back for two Christmas Specials in 2005. Syd has directed every single episode and they really all do it for him. So do we.

'Michael and Finty were absolutely mad about it – "a Bond-woman"'

The premiere of *Tomorrow Never Dies*

I never thought about what a huge responsibility I had in playing 'M'. I think
I was just really excited about it, and Michael and Finty were absolutely mad about
it — 'a Bond-woman.' It was lovely working with Pierce Brosnan. I didn't get to any
exotic locations, not in four Bond films. All I got was Stowe School, very nice but
not abroad, and I got a trailer labelled Innsbruck. I call this picture 'Guess who's
smallest?' Look how tall those girls are! But then Pierce and I are furthest away
from the camera.

Queen Victoria arriving at Balmoral in *Mrs Brown*

If Billy Connolly was nervous there was no sign of it. He was just fantastic from the word go. At the end of a day's filming we'd all go off for showers, then we'd meet in the bar and have a drink, and Billy would sit down with a pot of tea on a tray in front of him, and then sometimes he'd just start telling stories. I would be looking at my watch and thinking, 'Can I do tomorrow's filming on just five and a half hours' sleep?' We'd be absolutely weeping with laughter, and I'd look at my watch again and think, 'Can I do it on four and a half hours?'

Dancing at the Ghillies Ball

Half the local gentry turned out to play the staff
at Balmoral, as the extras had to be able to dance
the Eightsome Reels expertly. Billy danced it as if
to the manner born.

'We'd be absolutely weeping with
laughter, and I'd look at my watch
again and think, "Can I do it on four
and a half hours' sleep?"'

The most difficult scene in the film

It took twenty-one takes because the horses misbehaved, and my heavy skirts kept getting caught on the pommel as Billy lifted me down, and then our radio-mikes became entangled. It was a very important scene too, as it's their closest moment in the entire film, when the Queen refuses to let John Brown resign:

'I cannot allow it because I cannot live without you. Without you, I cannot find the strength to be who I must be.'

John Madden, the director, watches us rehearse the scene

'It took twenty-one takes because the horses misbehaved, and my heavy skirts kept getting caught on the pommel as Billy lifted me down'

Overleaf 'Without you, I cannot find the strength to be who I must be'
Pages 174 – 5 Duty calls – leaving Balmoral to return to public life as the Queen

10

More Screen-scenes
From *Shakespeare in Love* to *Mrs Henderson Presents*

Suddenly I was being offered more films than plays. Once again I felt I was following in Peggy Ashcroft's footsteps, who also enjoyed a late-flowering career in the cinema. But like her, too, I have no intention of abandoning the stage.

Elizabeth I in *Shakespeare in Love*

I wrote to John Madden after *Mrs Brown* and said to him, 'If ever there's a part of somebody just walking across the back, please can I do it?' He wrote to me saying, 'There is actually a part of somebody walking across the back.' It was only Elizabeth I! Because I had to look Gwyneth Paltrow straight in the eye, I had to have enormously high shoes, which were known as Tudor Spices. Some shots worked absolutely wonderfully, then John Madden would say, 'No, we'll have to go again.'

'Why?'

'A touch of the Tudor Spices there.'

'Because I had to look Gwyneth Paltrow
straight in the eye, I had to have
enormously high shoes, which were
known as Tudor Spices'

'I never expected to win the Oscar'

I feel for only eight minutes on the screen I should only get a little bit of him

I never expected to win the Oscar. Then, just before it was announced by Robin Williams, whom we'd met at Billy's, Michael squeezed my hand and said, 'Watch out, I think this is you.' I don't remember very much after that except Robin curtsying. I gave the Oscar to Michael to bring home and I went to the airport in Los Angeles, as I was flying to New York for *Amy's View*.

When he got back home he took Oscar to the pub!

Meeting Prince Charles at the
premiere of *Tea with Mussolini*
Flanked by Cher and Maggie Smith, with
the director Franco Zeffirelli far right.

Tea with Mussolini

It was the first time I worked with Joan Plowright and we became great friends (above left).

The dog always looked at its trainer off-set whichever way we were looking in front of the camera (above).

Off-set on *Tea with Mussolini*

Finty and Sammy came out to Italy to join me, and
we all took it in turns pushing the pram in the evening.

Iris Murdoch in *Iris* with Jim Broadbent as John Bayley

Jim and I had a very similar sense of the absurd,
and we laughed a lot between takes, which actually
helped us to play some of those scenes.

I discovered that we shared a love of cats. His was
called Naughty and I said, 'Oh, what a great name
for a cat.'

'Not so hot when you're sitting in the vet's
waiting-room with a whole lot of people, and they
come out and call Naughty Broadbent!'

It was wonderful when he won the Oscar for best
supporting actor, there was a lot of excitement in
our corner.

'It was quite difficult to play, because Iris Murdoch is so recently in our minds and everyone in the world seemed to have met her – except me'

The poster for *Iris*

What it misses there is Hugh Bonneville's name, who played John Bayley when young. He and Jim fused so seamlessly that a lot of people didn't realise there were two actors in the part.

With Kate Winslet in *Iris*

Kate Winslet played Iris Murdoch when young, so we had no scenes together except a time-switching shot under water. Left, at the premiere with Kate, and the first time I met John Bayley.

'I couldn't get into any car to go up from the car park to the house, because my hat was so high, so they gave me a wonderful golf buggy'

Lady Bracknell in *The Importance of Being Earnest*

The costumes were incredible. I was wearing two foxes who looked as if they were having a fight over my shoulders. I couldn't get into any car to go up from the car park to the house, because my hat was so high, so they gave me a wonderful golf buggy. One of the locals must have seen me, because a friend of Geoffrey Palmer's, Ivor Herbert, sent me a copy of the parish magazine which recorded in its diary:

Spotted at West Wycombe:
5 Buzzards riding the wind over village (23 May)
Fox crossing West Wycombe Hill Road, A4010 side, 8.45am (24 May)
Bar-Headed Geese, Lang Meadow (28 May)
Heard Cuckoo in flight, West Wycombe Hill, 8.30am (31 May)
Long-eared owl, A4010 side of West Wycombe Hill (3 June)
Dame Judi Dench in costume, main gate of Park (6 June)
Stoat chasing rabbit in the cricket meadow (8 June)

I loved the billing – after the long-eared owl, but before the stoat.

With Billy Connolly and John Hurt at the BAFTA Fellowship evening

When I won the BAFTA Best Actress Award for *Mrs Brown* in 1998, it was stolen even before I had left the hotel at the end of the evening. BAFTA replaced it so quickly I wondered if this happened all the time. It just shows you can't be too careful.

With Kevin Spacey at the premiere of *The Shipping News*

I've never had trouble with a bottle of champagne until then. Kevin Spacey was no help on this occasion!!

'I was very worried about this, but Billy Connolly and Jim Broadbent made it easier by sending me up rotten'

With Richard Eyre at the
BAFTA Fellowship Award evening in 2001

I was very worried about this, but Billy Connolly and Jim Broadbent made it easier by sending me up rotten. Jim said he hoped he had got my career back on track with *Iris* and described discovering what he called, 'the real Judi. Who of you knew, for instance, that she is over six foot tall and massively built? How many of you are aware that her strong Birmingham-Russian accent, which she so valiantly struggles to overcome in her stage and screen work, is in real life almost impenetrable? And it is a mark of her extreme professionalism that it was the very last week of filming before I even realised she had a prosthetic limb.'

I'm glad there were a few jokers. Mind you, quite a lot of Billy's jokes had to be edited out before the show could be broadcast.

With Maggie Smith in *Ladies in Lavender*

Charles Dance was so assured that you would never
have known this was his first film as director.
The young Polish violinist we rescued from the sea-
shore in Cornwall was played by a very good German
actor, Daniel Brühl, and this photograph was taken by
his interpreter, Georgia Oetker.

Ladies in Lavender

With Charles Dance and Maggie Smith at the premiere of *Ladies in Lavender,* Odeon Leicester Square, 8 November 2004.

With Maggie Smith

After our early years at the Old Vic Maggie and I only worked together at long intervals until recently, when we have done a play and two films in rapid succession.

'I had never worked with Bob before, it was a complete joy'

With Bob Hoskins in *Mrs Henderson Presents*

I had never worked with Bob before, it was a complete joy.
I had worked for Stephen Frears several times, and I so
enjoyed making this film that I never wanted it to end. I
played the woman who bought the Windmill Theatre and
employed Vivian van Damm, played by Bob.

11

Some Off-Duty Moments
'There aren't enough hours in the day for me'

There really aren't for me. You don't have to retire
as an actor. With any luck, there are all those parts
you can play lying in bed, or in wheelchairs; like
Newton Blick, he came off-stage and died in his
dressing-room. Lucky Newty, I say.

With Michael at the reopening of the Shakespeare Birthplace Trust in 2000

With Raymond Mander and Joe Mitchenson

I met them when I was at the Old Vic, and they used to take me to the Players Theatre and lots of First Nights. They were hugely good fun and they took me everywhere. Their house was full of theatrical treasures, and they let me hold the Order of the Elephant that Macready wore round his neck as Hamlet, which you can see in that wonderful portrait of him. They were so sweet, and they knew absolutely everybody. I was with them the night I first met Michael, when he was in *Celebration* at the Duchess Theatre; he came to join us in the pub afterwards in Covent Garden.

It was through them that I met the Edwardian actress Ada Reeve, who was a friend of Ray's and Joe's.

'They were so sweet, and they knew absolutely everybody. I was with them the night I first met Michael'

Greeting Princess Diana at the National Theatre

The ABSA Awards (Association for Business Sponsorship of the Arts) are usually held at the National, and often the Guest of Honour is a member of the Royal Family. As members of the National Theatre Company at the time, Edward Petherbridge and I were presented to the Princess of Wales in 1998.

The aqua-ballet

That's me on the right. We have always done lots of aqua-ballets, from the Nottingham West African tour in the mid-Sixties, at the big pool in Kaduna when we completely emptied the pool of people, to another on a rough day in the sea at Dubrovnik, while we were on tour with *Hamlet* with the National Theatre.

8 12'89

'We have always done lots of aqua-ballets'

With Cathleen Nesbitt at the Savoy Hotel
This was not long after I was married, at a cocktail party at the Savoy.
She was so beautiful, and you can see why Rupert Brooke wrote all
those letters to her.

'She was so beautiful, and you
can see why Rupert Brooke
wrote all those letters to her'

'I am 16, going on 17' with Brendan O'Hea
We developed this as our cabaret act for the party after the
last night of *A Little Night Music* at the National, and then we
did it at this club near Seven Dials for the charity West End
Cares. We had a very good time, but we mustn't do it any
more, because I am now 16 going on 70, as Brendan keeps
reminding me.

With Michael at John Mills's eightieth birthday, 1988

Johnny Mills was an incorrigible practical joker, worse than me. When we were in the musical of *The Good Companions* together, there was an actor in the company who was not behaving very well, so Johnny suggested that we put stage weights in his suitcase for the Going Away number. He couldn't lift the suitcase, let alone swing it about. John and I were both told we were amateurs. The night he and Mary invited Michael and me to join him for supper at Overton's after the show he caught me by surprise when he handed me the menu on-stage to place my order in advance, as the kitchens would be closed when we got there.

I told those stories at his memorial service in June 2005, which was a very nostalgic occasion, as we all remembered what a lovely man he was.

New Year's Eve 1987
The year I got my DBE, with our friends Susie and Gerald Bodmer.

With Finty at the TONY Awards in New York, 6 June 1999
I won the TONY (the Antoinette Perry Award) for *Amy's View* on Broadway. Finty came over and we all got ready in my dressing-room at the Barrymore Theater.

At the Oxford Union, 1 March 2002

This was such good fun in the end, except it was frightening.
I was so worried that I would be asked all sorts of highly
intellectual questions that I said I would only do it if I could
bring my biographer with me to take the chair. Then
the first question from the floor was 'Who's your favourite
James Bond?' and I thought this is going to be all right after all.

'Then the first question from the floor was "Who's your favourite James Bond?" and I thought this is going to be all right after all'

Guess what I'm thinking?
In a minute I'm going to ask John what I did, what was the play, what was the part and what was the date?

Ian Richardson makes me laugh

We had just taken part in a big fund-raising gala for
the Yvonne Arnaud Theatre in Guildford in 1996.
The rehearsal seemed to go on for ever and didn't
end until 6.30 p.m.

So I went all round the dressing-rooms,
collecting guesses at fifty pence a go, on what time
the actual gala performance would finish. Then we
had a party on-stage afterwards, and it looks here as
if Ian might have won the jackpot.

'I went all round the dressing
rooms, collecting guesses at
fifty pence a go'

Ian Richardson makes everyone laugh

We were all involved in *Men in Scarlet*, the son et lumière about the Chelsea Pensioners in 2000. At the press conference on the opening night one young man asked unwisely why we had all bothered to take part in such a show, and Ian barked back, 'Because these men are all heroes!' He was in sparkling form and kept us all amused as you can see.

Below, left to right John Miller (producer), Ian Richardson, Martin Jarvis, Sir Jeremy Mackenzie (Governor of the Royal Hospital) and a helpless me

Reopening the Shakespeare Birthplace Trust in 2000

That was such a lovely day. Michael and I went back to Stratford so often after we had moved away, we spent so many happy years there; and we were thrilled to be asked to cut the ribbon on this occasion, even if that proved a little more difficult in practice than we had anticipated (previous pages).

At Buckingham Palace

With Finty and Michael the day I received my DBE.

Shall I drive off into the sunset?
This is a very flash photo of me and my very flash car. I don't drive it. I just lean against it. It makes me feel about twenty-nine.

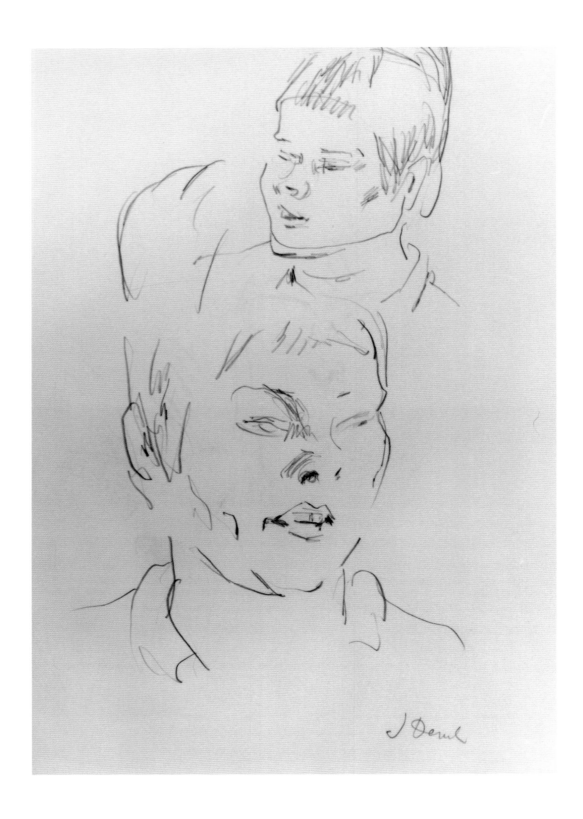

Portraits in the
National Portrait Gallery
Two portraits – sketch by Cecil Beaton 1969,
oil painting by Alessandro Raho 2004,
both at the National Portrait Gallery.

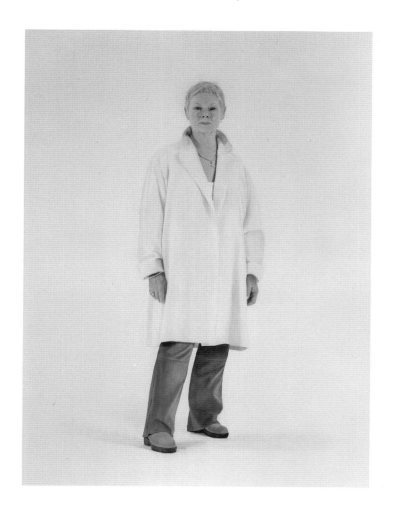

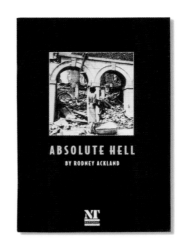

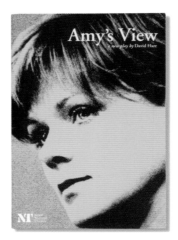

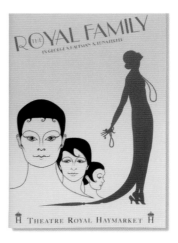

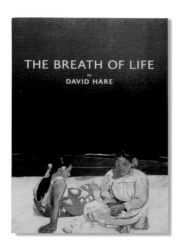

A random selection
of recent theatre
programmes

The Royal family in rehearsal

All's Well That Ends Well in rehearsal

CHRONOLOGY OF PARTS

THEATRE

Date	Play	Role	Theatre
1957	*York Mystery Plays*	Virgin Mary	St Mary's Abbey

The Old Vic Company, 1957–61

Date	Play	Role	Theatre
1957	*Hamlet*	Ophelia	Old Vic
	Measure for Measure	Juliet	Old Vic
	A Midsummer Night's Dream	First Fairy	Old Vic
1958	*Twelfth Night*	Maria	Old Vic
	Henry V (Both plays also on tour to North America)	Katharine	Old Vic
1959	*The Double Dealer*	Cynthia	Old Vic
	As You Like It	Phebe	Old Vic
	The Importance of Being Earnest	Cecily	Old Vic
	The Merry Wives of Windsor	Anne Page	Old Vic
1960	*Richard II*	Queen	Old Vic
	Romeo and Juliet (Also Venice Festival)	Juliet	Old Vic
	She Stoops to Conquer	Kate Hardcastle	Old Vic
	A Midsummer Night's Dream	Hermia	Old Vic
	(And walk-ons in *King Lear* and *Henry VI*)		

The Royal Shakespeare Company, 1961–2

Date	Play	Role	Theatre
1961	*The Cherry Orchard*	Anya	Aldwych
1962	*Measure for Measure*	Isabella	Stratford
	A Midsummer Night's Dream	Titania	Stratford
	A Penny for a Song	Dorcas Bellboys	Aldwych

The Nottingham Playhouse Company, 1963

Date	Play	Role	Theatre
1963	*Macbeth*	Lady Macbeth	Nottingham
	Twelfth Night (Both plays also on tour to West Africa)	Viola	Nottingham
	A Shot in the Dark	Josefa Lautenay	Lyric

The Oxford Playhouse Company, 1964–5

Date	Play	Role	Theatre
1964	*Three Sisters*	Irina	Oxford
	The Twelfth Hour	Anna	Oxford
1965	*The Alchemist*	Dol Common	Oxford
	Romeo and Jeannette	Jeannette	Oxford
	The Firescreen	Jacqueline	Oxford

The Nottingham Playhouse Company, 1965–6

Date	Play	Role	Theatre
1965	*Measure for Measure*	Isabella	Nottingham
	Private Lives	Amanda	Nottingham
1966	*The Country Wife*	Margery Pinchwife	Nottingham
	The Astrakhan Coat	Barbara	Nottingham
	St Joan	Joan	Nottingham

The Oxford Playhouse Company, 1966–7

Date	Play	Role	Theatre
1966	*The Promise*	Lika	Oxford
	The Rules of the Game	Silia	Oxford
1967	*The Promise*	Lika	Fortune
1968	*Cabaret*	Sally Bowles	Palace

The Royal Shakespeare Company, 1969–71

Date	Play	Role	Theatre
1969	*The Winter's Tale*	Hermione/Perdita	Stratford
	Women Beware Women	Bianca	Stratford
	Twelfth Night	Viola	Stratford
1970	*London Assurance*	Grace Harkaway	Aldwych

1971	*Major Barbara*	Barbara Undershaft	Aldwych
	The Merchant of Venice	Portia	Stratford
	The Duchess of Malfi	Duchess	Stratford
	Toad of Toad Hall	Fieldmouse, Stoat and Mother Rabbit	Stratford
1973	*Content to Whisper*	Aurelia	Royal, York
	The Wolf (Also at Apollo, Queen's & New London)	Vilma	Playhouse, Oxford
1974	*The Good Companions*	Miss Trant	Her Majesty's
1975	*The Gay Lord Quex*	Sophy Fullgarney	Albery

The Royal Shakespeare Company, 1975–80

1975	*Too True to be Good*	Sweetie Simpkins	Aldwych
1976	*Much Ado About Nothing*	Beatrice	Stratford
	Macbeth (Also Donmar and Young Vic)	Lady Macbeth	Stratford
	The Comedy of Errors	Adriana	Stratford
	King Lear	Regan	Stratford
1977	*Pillars of the Community*	Lona Hessel	Aldwych
1978	*The Way of the World*	Millamant	Aldwych
1979	*Cymbeline*	Imogen	Stratford
1980	*Juno and the Paycock*	Juno Boyle	Aldwych
1981	*A Village Wooing*	Young woman	New End

The National Theatre Company, 1982

1982	*The Importance of Being Earnest*	Lady Bracknell	Lyttelton
	A Kind of Alaska	Deborah	Cottesloe
1983	*Pack of Lies*	Barbara Jackson	Lyric

The Royal Shakespeare Company, 1984–5

1984	*Mother Courage*	Mother Courage	Barbican
1985	*Waste*	Amy O'Connell	Barbican and Lyric
1986	*Mr and Mrs Nobody*	Carrie Pooter	Garrick

The National Theatre Company, 1987–91

1987	*Antony and Cleopatra*	Cleopatra	Olivier
	Entertaining Strangers	Sarah Eldridge	Cottesloe
1989	*Hamlet*	Gertrude	Olivier
	The Cherry Orchard	Ranevskaya	Aldwych
1991	*The Plough and the Stars*	Bessie Burgess	Young Vic
	The Sea	Mrs Rafi	Lyttelton
1992	*Coriolanus*	Volumnia	Chichester

The Royal Shakespeare Company, 1992

| 1992 | *The Gift of the Gorgon* | Helen Damson | Barbican and Wyndham's |

The National Theatre Company, 1994–8

1994	*The Seagull*	Arkadina	Olivier
1995	*Absolute Hell*	Christine Foskett	Lyttelton
	A Little Night Music	Desireé Armfeldt	Olivier
1997	*Amy's View*	Esmé	Lyttelton
1998	*Amy's View*	Esmé	Aldwych
	Filumena	Filumena	Piccadilly
1999	*Amy's View*	Esmé	Barrymore, New York
2001	*The Royal Family*	Fanny Cavendish	Theatre Royal, Haymarket
2002	*The Breath of Life*	Frances	Theatre Royal, Haymarket
2003	*All's Well That Ends Well*	The Countess	Swan, Stratford-upon-Avon, and Gielgud

DIRECTOR

Date	Title	Company/Venues
1988	*Much Ado About Nothing*	Renaissance Theatre Company
1989	*Look Back in Anger*	Renaissance Theatre Company
	Macbeth	Central School of Speech and Drama
1991	*The Boys from Syracuse*	Regent's Park Open Air Theatre
1993	*Romeo and Juliet*	Regent's Park Open Air Theatre

TELEVISION

Date	Title	Company
1959	*Family on Trial*	Associated Rediffusion
1960	*Z-Cars*	BBC
	Henry V – Age of Kings	BBC
1962	*Major Barbara*	BBC
1963	*The Funambulists*	ATV
1965	*Safety Man – Mogul*	BBC
1966	*Talking to a Stranger*	BBC
1968	*On Approval*	Yorkshire
1970	*Confession – Neighbours*	Granada
1972	*Luther*	BBC
1973	*Keep an Eye on Amelie*	BBC
1977	*The Comedy of Errors* (RSC)	Thames
1978	*Macbeth* (RSC)	Thames
	Langrishe Go Down	BBC
	A Village Wooing	Yorkshire
1979	*On Giant's Shoulders*	BBC
	Love in a Cold Climate	Thames
1980–3	*A Fine Romance*	London Weekend
1980	*The Cherry Orchard*	BBC
	Going Gently	BBC
1982	*Saigon – Year of the Cat*	Thames
1985	*The Browning Version*	BBC
	Mr & Mrs Edgehill	BBC
	Ghosts	BBC
1986	*Make and Break*	BBC
1988	*Behaving Badly*	Channel 4
1990	*Can You Hear Me Thinking?*	BBC
	The Torch	BBC
1991	*Absolute Hell*	BBC
1991 –2002	*As Time Goes By*	BBC
1999	*The Last of the Blonde Bombshells*	BBC

FILMS

Date	Title	Director
1964	*The Third Secret*	Charles Crichton
1965	*He Who Rides a Tiger*	Charles Crichton
	A Study in Terror	James Hill
	Four in the Morning	Anthony Simmons
	A Midsummer Night's Dream	Peter Hall
1973	*Dead Cert*	Tony Richardson
1984	*Wetherby*	David Hare
1985	*A Room with a View*	James Ivory
1986	*84 Charing Cross Road*	David Jones
1987	*A Handful of Dust*	Charles Sturridge
1988	*Henry V*	Kenneth Branagh
1994	*Jack and Sarah*	Tim Sullivan
1995	*Goldeneye*	Martin Campbell
	Hamlet	Kenneth Branagh
1996	*Mrs Brown*	John Madden
1997	*Tomorrow Never Dies*	Roger Spottiswoode
1998	*Shakespeare in Love*	John Madden
1999	*Tea with Mussolini*	Franco Zeffirelli
	The World is Not Enough	Michael Apted
2000	*Chocolat*	Lasse Hallström
2001	*The Shipping News*	Lasse Hallström
	Iris	Richard Eyre
	The Importance of Being Earnest	Oliver Parker
2002	*Die Another Day*	Lee Tamahori
2004	*Ladies in Lavender*	Charles Dance
	The Chronicles of Riddick	Vin Diesel
2005	*Mrs Henderson Presents*	Stephen Frears

PICTURE CREDITS

Every effort has been made to trace or contact all copyright holders. The publishers would be pleased to rectify any errors or omissions brought to their attention at the earliest opportunity.

A number of the pictures have come from personal collections of the author and the editor. For kindly supplying other photographs we are grateful to: Tina Carr, Charles Dance, Laurence Guittard, David Hare, Barbara Leigh-Hunt, Georgia Oetker, Michael Pennington, John Reynolds, Ian Richardson, Anne Rowen, Clare Brown and Duncan Best at BAFTA, Richard Mangan at the Mander and Mitchenson Collection, Shona Robertson at the National Theatre Archive, Mark Dorrington of the Nottingham City Council Archive, Sylvia Morris and Helen Hargest at the Shakespeare Centre, Stratford-upon-Avon, Mairi MacDonald at the Shakespeare Birthplace Trust, Eddie Gallacher and the Oxford Union, Mark Tillie, John Timbers and Stanley Wells. In addition we would like to thank the following for permission to reproduce their pictures:

P 1–2 Judi Dench; 7 Carolyn Djanogly; 10 Barbara Leigh-Hunt; 12–13 Judi Dench; 14–15 Tina Carr; 16–17 Press Association; 18–23 Judi Dench; 24 (top) Yorkshire Post; 24 (bottom)–25 Judi Dench; 26 (left) David O'Neill / The Mail on Sunday; 26 (right) Judi Dench; 27 John Timbers; 28–33 Judi Dench; 34 John Timbers; 35– 40 Judi Dench; 41 John Timbers; 42–4 (top) Judi Dench; 44 (bottom) Tenniel Evans; 45–7 Judi Dench; 48 Wendy Toye; 49 Alec McCowen; 50 Judi Dench; 51 Crispian Woodgate 52–3 Judi Dench; 54 Gordon Goode / Shakespeare Birthplace Trust; 56 John Timbers; 57 Joe Cocks studio collection / Shakespeare Birthplace Trust; 58 Ian Richardson / Joe Cocks Studio Collection; 59 Zoë Dominic; 60–61 Nottingham Playhouse / Nottingham Archives; 62–67 Judi Dench; 68 Rex Features Ltd; 69 Zoë Dominic; 70–72 Joe Cocks studio collection / Shakespeare Birthplace Trust; 73 Ian Richardson / Joe Cocks Studio Collection; 74 Zoë Dominic; 75–76 Morris Newcombe; 77 (top) John Timbers; 77 (bottom) Joe Cocks studio collection / Shakespeare Birthplace Trust; 78–9 Patrick Eagar; 80 (top) John Brook / Shakespeare Birthplace Trust; 80 (bottom) Judi Dench; 81 John Brook / Shakespeare Birthplace Trust; 82 Donaldcooper @photostage.co.uk; 84–85 Zoë Dominic; 86–7 Nobby Clark; 88–9 Joe Cocks studio collection / Shakespeare Birthplace Trust; 90 Solihull News; 91 Joe Cocks studio collection / Shakespeare Birthplace Trust; 92–3 Donaldcooper@photostage.co.uk; 94 Sally Soames / The Sunday Times; 95 Donaldcooper @photostage.co.uk; 96–7 Joe Cocks studio collection / Shakespeare Birthplace Trust; 98 Zoë Dominic; 100 Donaldcooper@photostage.co.uk; 101 Judi Dench; 102–4 Zoë Dominic; 105 Laurence Burns; 106 Donaldcooper @photostage.co.uk; 107–8 Nobby Clark; 109 Reg Wilson / Royal Shakespeare Company; 110 John Haynes; 112 Radio Times; 113 Granada Television; 114 John Haynes; 115 Douglas H. Jeffrey; 116 Donaldcooper@photostage.co.uk; 117 Nobby Clark; 118–123 (top) John Haynes; 123 (bottom) Judi Dench; 124 Mark Douet; 126 Robbie Jack; 127 Mark Douet; 129 John Haynes; 130 Richard Mildenhall; 131 Reg Wilson / Rex Features; 132 (top) Radio Times; 132–3 John Timbers; 134 Royal National Theatre, UK. Photography by Martin Norris; 135 John Haynes; 136 Judi Dench; 137 Mark Douet; 138–140 John Haynes; 141 John Timbers; 142 Alistair Muir; 143 Malcolm Davies / Shakespeare Birthplace Trust; 144 Mark Tillie / Ecosse / Miramax; 146–7 Judi Dench; 148–9 David Hare; 150 Judi Dench; 151–3 John Timbers; 154 Judi Dench; 155 London Weekend Television / Rex Features; 156–60 DLT Entertainment UK Limited; 161 John Timbers; 162–3 DLT Entertainment UK Limited; 164–5 Judi Dench; 166–75 Mark Tillie / Ecosse / Miramax; 176 Rex Features; 178–9 Everett Collection / Rex Features; 181 R. Hepler / Everett / Rex Features; 182 (top) AKG Images; 182 (bottom) Rex Features; 183 Everett Collection / Rex Features; 184 Judi Dench; 185–6 Rex Features; 187 AKG Images; 188 Greg Williams / Art and Commerce; 190–2 BAFTA; 193 Georgia Oetker; 194 The Moviestore Collection; 195 Richard Young / Rex Features; 196–7 Stephen Frears; 198 News-Team Syndication; 200 Daily Express / Mander and Mitchenson Theatre Collection; 201 Tomas Jaski Ltd / Mander and Mitchenson Theatre Collection; 202 Bill Mackenzie / National Theatre Archive; 203–7 Judi Dench; 208–9 Eddie Gallacher and the Oxford Union; 210 Ian Richardson; 211 John Miller; 212–13 News-Team Syndication; 214–5 Judi Dench; 216–7 The National Portrait Gallery, London; 218 Copyright of the Royal National Theatre, UK, the RSC, the Peter Hall Company and the Theatre Royal Haymarket. Photography by Martin Norris; 219 (top) Copyright of the Peter Hall Company, Theatre Royal Haymarket, (bottom) the RSC. Photography by Martin Norris. 224 Camera Press.

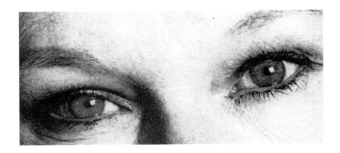

First published in Great Britain in 2005
by Weidenfeld & Nicolson
10 9 8 7 6 5 4 3 2 1

A CIP catalogue record for this book is available from
the British Library.

ISBN-13:   978 0 297 84427 3
ISBN-10:   0 297 84427 X

Design director: David Rowley
Designed by Clive Hayball
Picture research by Brónagh Woods
Editorial by Anna Hervé and Jennie Condell

Printed and bound in Great Britain by Butler and Tanner

Weidenfeld & Nicolson
The Orion Publishing Group Ltd
Wellington House
125 Strand
London WC2R 0BB

The Orion Publishing Group's policy is to use papers that are
natural, renewable and recyclable products and made from wood
grown in sustainable forests. The logging and manufacturing
processes are expected to conform to the environmental
regulations of the country of origin.